Bachelor Comfort Food

REGIS J. BELCHER JR.

Bachelor Comfort Food
Copyright © 2023 by Regis J. Belcher Jr.

ISBN: 978-1962497152 (sc)
ISBN: 978-1962497169 (e)

The views expressed in this book are solely those of the author and do not necessarily reflect the views of the publisher, and the publisher hereby disclaims any responsibility for them.

The Reading Glass Books
(888) 420-3050
www.readingglassbooks.com
production@readingglassbooks.com

IN LOVING MEMORY

OF MY WIFE

Barbara

and

My son Reggie III

Table of Contents

DESSERT

MEASUREMENT

BREAKFAST

Let's cook

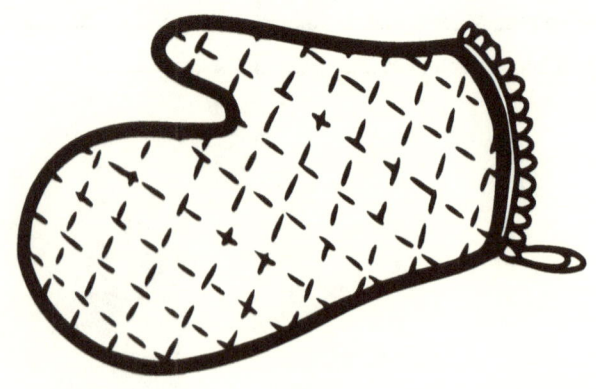

Buttermilk Biscuits and Sausage Gravy

Buttermilk Biscuits

2 ½ Cups self-rising flour (plus extra for flouring your surface)

2 Tsp sugar (optional)

½ Tsp Kosher salt

4 Tbsp Vegetable shortening (see baking tips below)

4 Tbsp butter (chilled)

1 chilled buttermilk (plus 1-2 more, if needed)

1Tbsp melted butter (optional: to brush on top of the biscuits)

Sausage Gravy

1 lb sage-flavored pork sausage

¼ Cup finely chopped white or yellow onion

6 Tbsp all purpose flour

4 Cups whole milk

½ Tsp Poultry seasoning (optional)

½ Tsp nutmeg (optional)

¼ Tsp kosher salt

1-2 dash of Worcestershire

1-2 dash of Tabasco or other hot sauce

1-2 Tbsp butter or bacon grease

Directions

Buttermilk biscuits

1. Baking Tip 1.) Spoon the flour into your measuring cup, and level it off with the back side of a knife. If you scoop the flour, it will pack into the measuring cup, yielding too much flour, 2.) Instead of 4 Tbsp each of butter and shortening, feel free to use 8 Tbsp each of butter or shortening or any combination up to 8 Tbsp.

2. Preheat oven to 450 degree a floured surface for shaping the dough and have an ungreased baking sheet ready (lined with silpat sheets if you have them).

3. Whisk together flour, sugar and salt in a medium-size bowl. Using a fork or a pastry blender cut in shortening and butter. Work quickly, you don't want the fat to melt—the key to fluffy biscuits is minimal handing. The mixture should be crumbly.

4. Make a well in the mixture, and pour in the buttermilk. Stir with a spoon and blend just until the liquid is absorbed and the dough comes away from sides of the bowl—add 1-2 tbsp more buttermilk if the dough is dry. Do not over mix; the dough will be tacky, neither wet nor dry.

5. With lightly floured hands, turn out the dough onto a lightly-floured surface and gently fold it over on itself 2 or 3 times. Shape into a ¾ thick round. If you use a rolling pin, bee sure to flour it first to keep the dough from sticking to the pin.

6. Using a 2-inch biscuits cutter, cut out the biscuits pressing straight down (avoid the temptation to twisting the cutter as twisting keeps the biscuits from rising). Dip the cutter in flour between cutting to keep the dough from sticking to the cutter. Place biscuits on the baking sheet so that they just touch (crunchy sides, leave space in between). Reshape scrap dough and continue cutting. Remember to handle the dough as little as possible.

7. Bake for 15-18 minutes or until golden brown on top. Turn the baking sheet around halfway through baking.

Optional: Brush the tops of the biscuits with melted butter.

Sausage gravy

1. Preheat a 4-quart saucepan over medium high heat (put a few drops of water in the pan—when they evaporate, you know the pan is ready). Crumble the sausage into the pan and let it brown for a minutes or two, then turn down to medium heat. Continue cooking, breaking up the sausage into smaller places, until no pink remains. Stir in the onion and cook until they are transparent.

2. Remove sausage with a slotted spatula or spoon, leaving the drippings in the pan. If less than 3 tbsp of drippings remain, add enough butter (or bacon grease) to equal about 3 tbsp of drippings. Add the sausage back to the pan on medium heat, and sprinkle the flour over the sausage. Stir in the flour and cook for about 6-8 minutes, until the mixture start bubbling and turns slightly golden brown.

3. Stir in poultry seasoning, Worcestershire sauce, Tabasco sauce and salt— cook for 1 minute to deepen the flavors. Slowly add the milk and cook over medium heat, stirring occasionally, until thickened (about15 minutes). Be patient, it will thicken!

Yield: Makes 10-12 servings

Eggs Benedict

Ingredients

2 English muffins, halved horizontally

4 Slices Canadian bacon

4 **Eggs** for poaching

2 Tablespoons distilled white vinegar

2 Teaspoons **Kosher salt**

Hollandaise sauce (see recipe below)

Garnish parsley or chives

Directions

1. Toast English muffin slices under the boiler or in the oven for approximately 3 minutes or until golden brown. Remove from boiler, spread with one teaspoon butter. In a large frying pan, cook Canadian bacon slices until lightly brown and place them on each English half.

2. Use a pan that is at least 3-inch deep so there is enough water to cover the eggs and they do not stick to the bottom of the pan. **NOTE: To prevent sticking, grease the pan with a little oil before filling vinegar and salt to the poaching water** ; bring the poaching water to a boil and reduce to a simmer before adding the eggs (bubbles should not break the surface). **Hint: When you poach eggs, adding a little vinegar and salt to the water will**

help the egg to hold its shape. Without it's the eggs will become skeins of protein tangling up in the water.

3. Break each egg onto a saucer or into small bowls. Slip eggs carefully into simmering water by lowering the lip of each egg-cup ½—below the surface of the water. Let the eggs flow out. Immediately cover with a lip and turn off the heat. Set timer for exactly three minutes for medium-firm yolks. Adjust the time up or down for runnier or firmer yolks. Cook 3-5

4. Remove from water with slotted spoon. Lift each perfectly poached egg from the water with slotted spoon, but hold over the water briefly to let any water clinging to the egg to drain off. Drain well before serving. Top each English muffin half with poached egg. Spoon warns hollandaise sauce over egg and garnished with a small parley sprig or chopped chive.

Variation Ideas: Substitute thinly sliced smoked salmon for the Canadian bacon.

Hollandaise Sauce

Ingredients

8 ounces unsalted clarified butter

3 Egg yolks

3 Tablespoon water

Juice of ½ lemon

Pinch of kosher salt and pepper

Directions

1. **Melt the butter over very low heat without** stirring and skim off the solids floating on top

2. **Fill a pan about half way with water and bring it** to just below boiling. Place the eggs yolk in a Pyrex bowl that fits just the pan

3. **Whisk in the three tablespoons of water and** place bowl in the pan of simmer water. Continually whisk until egg yolks thicken and lighten (about 5 minutes)

4. **Remove from heat and very gradually pour in** the clarified butter continually whisking

5. **Whisk in lemon juice and kosher salt and pepper** to taste

6. **Best served immediately or warm a few** seconds in the microwave. If the sauce is too thick you can whisk in a little hot water

Waffle

Ingredients

1 Cup all-propose flour

½ Teaspoon baking soda

1 Teaspoon baking power

1 teaspoon salt

3 tablespoon sugar

3 Egg beaten

2 ounce unsalted butter, melt

16 ounce buttermilk, (room temperature)

Vegetable spray, for the waffle iron

Directions

Preheat waffle iron

1. In a medium bowl whisk together the flour, soda, baking powder, and. In another bowl beat together eggs and melt butter, then add buttermilk. Add the wet ingredient to the wet ingredients to the dry and stir until combined. Allow to rest for 5 minutes

2. Ladle the recommended amount of waffle batter onto the iron according to the manufacturer's recommendations. Close iron top and cook until the waffle is golden brown on both sides and is easily removed from iron. Serve immediately or keep warn in a 200 degree oven until ready to serve

Old Fashioned Pancake

Ingredients

1 ½ Cups all-purpose flour

3 ½ Teaspoon baking powder

1 Teaspoon salt

1 Tablespoon white sugar

1 ¼ Cups milk

1 Egg

3 Tablespoons butter, melt

Directions

1. In a large bowl, sift together the flour, baking powder, salt and sugar. Make a well in the center and pour in the milk, egg and melted butter, mix until smooth

2. Heat a lightly oiled griddle or frying pan over medium high heat. Pour or scoop the batter onto the griddle, using approximately ¼ cup for each pancake. Brown on both sides and serve hot

SOUP

AND

SANDWICH

Bean Soup

Ingredients

1lb Bag great northern beans, sorted and soak overnight, rinsed

2lb Smoked ham bones

2 ½ Cups Water

2 Potatoes, peeled and cubed

1 Large carrot, peeled and large dice

2 Tablespoon olive oil

1 Tablespoon Ham stock (if you can't ham stock you can use chicken stock)

Salt and pepper to taste

1 Small onion finely chopped

1-2 Bay leaves

1 Cup tomato juice

½ Cup cream

1-3 clove of garlic crush

Directions

1. In a large stock pot, pour in quart of boiling water and let them soak for about one hour or overnight

2. While beans are draining, sweat the onion, garlic and carrots in olive oil

3. Add the water, tomato juice, drained beans, ham bones, salt, ham base (you are used ham base do not add salt)

4. Reduce heat to simmer, Stirring occasionally (uncovered) until beans until are soft and the meat is falls off of the bones

5. Remove the bones, cool, pick the meat off and put onto the soup

6. Add the diced potatoes, simmer (uncovered) another 15 minutes

7. Add the cream, taste broth adjust seasonings if needed

8. Continue to simmer until potatoes are cooked through and serve

Beef Barley Vegetable Soup

Ingredients

3lb Beef chuck roast

½ Cup barley

1 Bay leaf

2 tablespoon oil

3 carrots, chopped

1 onion, chopped

3 stalks celery chopped

16 ounce of fresh mixed vegetables (you can use frozen mixed vegetables)

4 Cups Beef stock

¼ Teaspoon ground black pepper

1 (28 ounce) can chopped stewed tomatoes

Salt and ground pepper to taste

Directions

1. In a stock pot cook chuck roast until very tender add barley and bay leaf during the last hour of cooking. Remove meat, and chop into bite-size pieces. Discard bay leaf. Set, broth, and barley aside

2. Heat oil in a large stock pot over medium-high heat. Sauté carrot, celery, onion and fresh or frozen mixed vegetable until tender. Add stock beef 1/4 Teaspoon pepper, chopped stewed tomatoes and beef/barley mixture. Bring to a boil, reduce heat and simmer for 10-20 minutes. Season with salt and pepper to taste

Chicken Noodle Soup

Ingredients

1 tablespoon olive oil

1 tablespoon butter

1 Cup carrots, peeled and sliced

3 Stalks celery, sliced

1 Medium onion, sliced

2 Quart chicken stock broth, low sodium preferred

3 Cups egg noodle, uncooked

3 Cups chicken meat and chopped into bite size bits

Handful parsley, chopped

Pinch salt and pepper

Directions

1. In a large stockpot. Melt butter with olive oil medium low heat. Add carrots, celery, onion, and a pinch of salt and pepper, and cook until veggie are tender, about 10 minutes

2. Add broth, turn heat to high and bring to a boil

3. Add egg noodle and cook for approximately 9 minutes, to until noodles are tender

4. Reduce heat to a gentle simmer, stir in chicken and parsley and cook for 5 minute more, or until chicken is heated through. Taste for seasonings and add more salt and pepper if needed

Chicken Vegetable Soup

Ingredients

1 (3pound) whole chicken

1 Onion, cut into thick slices

5 Stalks celery, thick slice

1 Tablespoon salt

1 Teaspoon fresh basil leaves packed

1 Teaspoon coarse ground black pepper

5 Carrots, sliced

2 Tablespoon chicken soup base

2 Cups uncooked egg noodles

Directions

1. Place chicken, onion, celery, salt, basil and pepper in a 10 quart stock pot. Fill stock pot with water until ingredients are fully covered and bring to a boil. Let simmer for 1 ½ hour or until chicken is tender

2. Remove chicken from pot with a slotted spoon and set aside

3. Add carrots, chicken soup base and uncooked noodles to the stock and increase temperature

4. While noodles and vegetables are cooking, tear chicken apart from bones. Cut up into pieces and add to soup in stock pot. Be sure to add additional water if ingredients are not fully covered. Bring to a boil, reduce to a simmer for about 10 minutes or just until noodles are cooked

Cream of Broccoli

Ingredients

3 Cups water

2 Teaspoons salt

1 Cup of Broccoli

2 Tablespoons butter

3 Tablespoon all propose flour

½ Cup Cream

1 Cup milk

1 ½ finely chopped onion

Salt and pepper to taste

Directions

1. In a medium saucepan, bring 3 cups water salt to a boil. Cook broccoli in boiling water, uncovered, for 10 to 12 minutes. Drain, place broccoli in a small bowl, and mash

2. Melt butter in a large saucepan over medium heat. Mix in flour, and then gradually whisk in milk and cream, water, stir continuously until liquid begins to boil. Stir in onion and mashed broccoli. Season with salt and white pepper

Place Potato Soup

Ingredients

4 Large Potatoes, Cubed

6 Stalks Celery, Chopped

1 Large Onion, Chopped

4 Cups water, or as needed

1 (12 fluid ounce) can evaporated milk

6 Tablespoons butter

Salt and ground pepper to taste

Directions

1. Place the potato cubes, celery, and onion into a pressure cooker and add 4 cups of water, or enough to reach the fullness mark on your cooker. (Follow manufacturer's directions for how full to fill your cooker.) Cover the cooker, seal, and bring the pressure up over medium heat. When cooker reaches full pressure, reduce heat to maintain the pressure, and pressure-cook the vegetables for 25 minutes.

2. Allow the pressure in the cooker to subside, and release the cover on the cooker when the pressure is normal. Mix in the evaporated milk, butter, salt, and black pepper, and bring the soup to a boil over medium heat. Reduce heat to a simmer, and cook the soup to the desired thickness, 5 to 15 minutes.

Classic Grilled Cheese Sandwich

Ingredients

4 slice white bread

3 Tablespoon butter (divided)

Directions

1. Preheat skillet over medium heat. Generously butter one side of a side of a slice of bread. Place bread butter-side-down onto skillet bottom and add 1 slice of cheese. Butter a second slice of bread on one side and place butterside-up on top of sandwich. Grill until lightly browned and flip over, continue grilling until cheeses melted. Repeat with remaining 2 slices of bread, butter and slice of cheese

Ham Salad Sandwich

Ingredients

2 Cups finely diced ham

3 Hard-boiled eggs chopped

¼ Cup sweet pickle relish

¼ Cup mayonnaise

2 Tablespoon minced onion

2 Tablespoon minced celery

2 Tablespoon minced red bell pepper

1 Tablespoon chopped fresh parsley

2 Teaspoon Dijon Mustard

1 Tablespoon lemon juice

A large pinch of cayenne (optional)

Kosher Salt and black pepper taste

Directions

1. Mix everything but the kosher salt, and cayenne in a large bowl. Taste and add cayenne, kosher salt and black pepper to taste. Serve chilled.

2. Serve straight, or mixed in with macaroni or in a sandwich hamburger bun, regular bread. Good with lemonade on a hot day

Yield 3-4 sandwiches

Hot Open Face Turkey Sandwich

Ingredients

1 ½ lb leftover turkey meat slice

½ Cup or so of leftover turkey gravy

Stock or water (to thin the gravy if needed)

4 large slice rustic bread

Directions

1. Heat gravy in a skillet until bubbly. If the gravy is too thick, thin with a little stock or water

2. Add pieces of slice cooked turkey meat to the gravy. Coat with the gravy on all sides and heat until the meat is heated through

3. Arrange a slice of bread (rustic French bread or Italian loaf would work great) on a plate. Top with sliced turkey and gravy

Yield serve 4

Tuna Salad Sandwich

Ingredients

1 (6 ounce) Can of tuna fish (if packed in water, drain it, and add a teaspoon of good quality olive oil)

2 Tablespoon of mayonnaise

¼ Purple onion, chopped finely

1 Celery stalk chopped finely

Juice of half of a lemon

Pinch or two of dill

2 tablespoon minced fresh parsley

1 Teaspoon Dijon mustard

Directions

Mix all of ingredient. Serve on toast, either open faced, or in a regular sandwich with lettuce. (For a low carb option, serve on bed lettuce)

Tomato Soup

Ingredients

2 Tablespoons butter or margarine

1 Tablespoon all-purpose flour

2 Cups tomato juice Tablespoon

½ Cup water

1/8 teaspoon salt

3/4 cup cooked wide egg noodle

Directions

1. In a saucepan over medium heat, melt butter. Add flour; stir to
   form a smooth paste. Gradually add tomato juice and water,
   stirring constantly, bring to a boil. Cook and stir for 2 minutes
   or thickened. Add salt stir in egg noodles and heat through

Vegetable Soup

Ingredients

1 Bunch celery, chopped

1 Medium head cabbage, chopped

1 Zucchini, chopped

6 Onions, chopped

8 Tomato, chopped

2 cloves garlic, minced

1-2 Bay leaf

1 quart beef stock

8 Peppercorn

Directions

In a large pot, combine celery, cabbage, zucchini, onion, and tomatoes. Pour in enough water to cover by one inch. Stir in beef stock, garlic, peppercorn and bay leaf. Bring to a boil, then reduce heat and simmer 90 minutes to 2 hours, until vegetable are tender and flavors are well blended.

MAIN COURSE

Brown Beef Stew

Ingredients

4 pound of beef stew meat, cut into 1 ½-inch cubes
2 Teaspoons kosher salt
Freshly ground black pepper
3 Tablespoon flour
3 Tablespoon vegetable oil
1 Large onion, halved and slices
1 Cup red wine
1 Cups plain tomato sauce or tomato puree
1 Cup broth beef
A sprig of thyme and a bay leaf
4 celery stalks cut into ½-inch pieces, their leave chopped
6 carrots and / or parsnip, peeled ½-inch pieces

Directions

1. Heat the oven to 325 degree

2. Season the meat very well with salt and pepper, and sprinkle the flour over all of it tossing the cubes to coat them. It's okay if some cubes and flourier or saltier the others, it well all even out in the pot

3. In a large Dutch oven heat half the oil over medium-high heat until hot but not smoking, then brown the meat well on as many sides as a reasonably possible. This is the only part of this dish that's a bit of the pan, and it just is what it is you will need to do the meat in batches, adding more oil at some point, because if you crowed it then it will steam instead of browning property. (I do

the meat in 2 ½ batches I add onion to the pan with the final half batch of meat and stir and brown then while the meat is doing its thing alongside. Tongs are good for flipping the meat over, and you can adjust the heat if the meat is either not browning property to if anything seems to be burning.)

4. Also—and I swear this the last thing I'm saying about this—I actually deglaze the pan between batches because otherwise the bottom of my pot seems to burn so after the batch of meat done, I pour half of the wine into the pot, swirl it around and scrape with a spatula to get up all the nice stuff from the bottom, then pour it into the dish with the already—brown meat and heat more oil for the second batch, which I do the same way honestly. You're talking about a twenty-five minutes investment in browning for measurable stew pleasure later on it's totally worth it)

5. Have you already browned the onions by now? If not, add another splash of oil to the pot and brown the onion for 5 or 10 minutes until they are nicely color. Add the meat and its juices back to the pot, along with whatever wine you haven't used yet, the tomato sauce, the broth, the herbs, and the remaining vegetables. Bring to a simmer over high heat, then press a large piece pf parchment down onto surface of the stew—the paper should come up far enough that the lid will hold it in place—and cover the pot with a heavy lid (if you don't have any parchment, slip this step, but expect to add more liquid at some point as more will evaporate)

6. Cook the e stew in the oven for 2 to 3 hours until the meat is fork tender, checking on it every now and again to make sure that the liquid isn't on the verge of being entirely evaporated if it is add more broth or a cup of water. After it's cooked taste the e stew and add salt if it needs it which it might or might not, depending on you broth. Serve in bowls or with buttered egg noodle or mashed potatoes

Buttermilk Fried Chicken

Ingredients

1 (3pound) fryer cut into pieces

2 Cups buttermilk

1 Large onion, sliced

¼ Cup chopped mixed fresh herbs (parsley, tarragon, Thyme) or a teaspoon each of dried herbs

½ Teaspoon paprika

½ Teaspoon cayenne pepper

2 Cups flour

½ Teaspoon garlic powder

½ Teaspoon onion powder

1 Teaspoon cayenne pepper

Kosher salt and pepper

2 Cups vegetable oil or canola oil other high smoke-point oil

Directions

1. Soak chicken overnight (at least 8 hours and up to two day) in buttermilk with onion, herbs, paprika, and cayenne pepper. (Regarding the use of buttermilk I have had good results from soaking chicken in plain yogurt instead of buttermilk.)

2. Drain in colander, leaving some herbs on chicken. In a large plastic (sturdy) bag, mix flour with seasoning. Meanwhile, heat 2 cups of oil in a large, heavy-bottom skillet Cast iron, stain steel— something that cab take the heat) on a medium high heat until a pinch of flour start to sizzle when dropped in the hot oil (but not so hot that the pan is smoking). **Remember when working with hot oil, always have a pan lid close by**

3. Place chicken pieces in bag with flour and shake until thoroughly coated. Add chicken to hot pan and fry on 1 side for 12-15 minutes, until golden brown, and then use tongs to turn chicken over and fry for another 10-12 minutes, again until golden brown. Be careful to keep the oil hot enough to fry chicken, but not so high as it burns the chicken. To do this on our electric stove we have to alternate the setting between high to medium high several times while we cooking

4. Use tongs to remove chicken from pan. Place on a rack over a cookie sheet or boiler pan for excess oil to drain. Add more kosher salt and pepper to taste

Yield serves 4

Chicken and Dumpling

Chicken and Vegetable:

Ingredients

4 pounds chicken thighs and breast parts, skin-on, bone-in

2 teaspoons butter or olive oil

Dash of salt

1 quart chicken stock (homemade is the best)

2 Celery stalks, trimmed and cut into ½-inch pieces

3 medium carrots, peeled and cut into ½-inch pieces

1 large onion, roughly chopped

6 Tbsp all-purpose flour

1 Teaspoon dried thyme

¼ Cup of sherry or vermouth (optional)

1 Tbsp of heavy cream (optional)

¾ Cup frozen peas, thawed

¼ Cup minced fresh parsley leaves

Ground black or white pepper

Dumplings:

Ingredients

2 Cups cake flour (can sub all-purpose flour, but use cake flour if you have it, your dumplings will be flutter.

2 Teaspoon baking powder

¾ Teaspoon kosher salt

2 Tbsp butter, melted

¾ Cup milk

Directions

1. Heat the chicken stock to a gentle in a medium pot.

2. In a separate, large pot, heat the butter or olive oil medium-high heat. Pat dries the chicken pieces and sprinkle with salt. Working in batches, brown the chicken pieces, placing the pieces skin-side down first; this will render out fat you will use to build the stew later

3. Once the chicken pieces are browned on both sides, remove them from the large pot, and turn off the heat. Remove and discard the skin from the chicken pieces and put the chicken pieces into the pot of simmer stock. Poach the chicken in the stock until cooked through, about 20 minutes or so. Remove the chicken pieces and set on a tray to cool for a few minutes. When the chicken pieces arte cool to tough, pull the meat off the bones and cut into 2-inch, set aside.

4. Return the heat on the large pot to medium-high. When it is hot, add the onion, celery, carrot and thyme and sauté until soft, but not brown, about 4-5 minutes. Add the flour and mix well. The flour will absorb all the fat in the pot and will stick a little to the bottom. Turn the heat to medium-low and stir this constantly for 2-3 minutes. Do not let it burn.

5. Get a ladler ready and have the of simmering chicken stock nearby. Add the sherry to flour vegetable mixture. It will sputter

and seize up. Add a ladle of hot chicken stock to and stir well. It will be goopy. Add another ladle, then another, stirring all the while, until the broth comes together. Add the rest of the chicken stock, the reserved chicken meat. Increase the heat and bring to a simmer, then reduce the heat to maintain a gentle while you make the dumplings.

6. Main the dumpling batter by sifting together flour, baking powder, and salt in a medium bowl. Add (optional) chopped fresh herbs. Add melted butter and milk to the dry ingredients. Gently mix with a wooden spoon until mixture just comes together. (Note: do not over mix! Or your dumpling will turn out too dense.)

7. Drop dumpling batter into the simmering stew by heaping teaspoonfuls, over the surface of the stew. (Note that the dumplings will easily double in size as they cook.) Cover and simmer until dumplings are cooked through, about 15 minutes. Once you have covered the pan, do not uncover and peek while the dumpling is cooking! In order for the dumplings to be light and fluffy, they must steam, not boil. Uncovering the pan releases the steam. If after 15 minutes they are still not cooked through (use a toothpick or skewer to test) cover pan again, and cook for another 5 to 10 minutes.

Yield: serves 6 to 8

Chicken Fried Steak

Ingredients

2-¼ Cups all-purpose flour, divided

¾ Teaspoon each salt, onion powder, chill pepper and pepper

2 eggs, lightly beaten

1-2/3 Cups buttermilk, divided

4 Beef cubed steak (4 ounces each)

Of oil for frying

1 ½ Cups 2% milk

Directions

1. In a shallow bowl, combine 2 cups flour, baking powder and seasonings. In another shallow bowl, combine egg and 1 cup buttermilk. Dip each cubed steak in buttermilk mixture, and then roll in flour mixture. Let stand for 5 minutes

2. In a large skillet heat ½ inch of oil on medium-heat. Fry steaks for 5-7 minutes. Turn carefully, cook 5 minutes longer or until coating is crisp meat is no longer pink. Remove steaks and keep warn 3. Drain reserving 1/3 cup drippings; stir remaining flour into drippings until smooth. Cook and stir over medium heat for 2 minutes. Gradually whisk in milk and buttermilk. Bring to a boil, cook and stir for 2 minutes or until thickened. Serve with steaks

Yield: 4 servings (2 cups gravy)

Classic Baked Chicken

Ingredients

3-4 lb chicken cut into 8 parts (2breasts, 2 thighs, 2 legs, 2 wings)
Excluding the back
Olive oil
Kosher Salt and freshly ground pepper
½ cups of chicken stock or white wine for the gravy (Optional)

Directions

1. Preheat oven to 400degree. Rinse chicken pieces in water and pat dry with paper towels. Coat the bottom of a roasting pan with olive oil. Rub some olive oil over all of the chicken pieces in the roasting pan. Sprinkle both sides of the chicken pieces with kosher salt and freshly ground pepper. Arrange the pieces skin-side up in the roasting pan so the largest pieces are in the center (breasts) and there is a little room between pieces so they aren't crowed in the pan

2. Cook for 30 minutes at 400 degree. Then lower the heat to 350 degree and cook for 10-30 minutes more (approximately 14-15 minutes per pound total cooking time) until juices run clear (not pink) then poked with a sharp knife or internal temperature of the chicken breasts is 165 degree and for the thighs 170 degree. If your chicken pieces aren't browning to your satisfaction, you can put them under the boiler for the last 5 minutes of cooking, until browned sufficiently

3. Remove roasting pan from the oven, Remove chicken from roasting pan to a serving plate. Tent with aluminum foil and let rest for 5 minutes before serving

Chicken gravy

1. To make gravy for the chicken, take the roasting pan with its drippings and place on a medium heat setting on the stovetop. Use a metal spatula to scrape up the drippings stuck to the bottom of the pan. Add a quarter cup of white wine or chicken stock* to the pan to help deglaze the drippings from the pan

2. Pour the wine/chicken stock and dripping mixture into a small saucepan and heat on medium high to reduce to desired thickness * While the chicken pieces are baking, if you bought a whole chicken that was then cut into pieces, you may have the back, the neck, and some gizzard pieces to use for making chicken stock. You can cut up the back a little, put it and the neck and gizzards (not the liver) into a saucepan, barely cover with water, and bring to simmer, cook while the chicken is cooking. When the chicken in the oven is done cooking, use the stock from simmering the extra pieces to make the gravy.

Yield: serves 4

Glazed Baked Ham

Ingredients

½ Ready-to-eat, cooked ham, bone-in, uncut (not spiral cut), shank end or butt end, about 9-11 pounds

Sweet hot honey mustard glaze

3 Tablespoon sweet hot honey mustard (or brown mustard with honey)

2 Tablespoon brown sugar

About 50 cloves

Honey Thyme glaze

3 Tablespoon melted butter

2 Tablespoon chopped fresh thyme

¼ Cup cider vinegar

¼ Cup honey

1 tablespoon sugar

1 Teaspoon Worcestershire sauce

Directions

1. Remove the ham from the refrigerator (still wrapped) a couple of hours before you intend to cook it can get closer to room temperature.

2. Preheat oven to 325 degree. Place ham, fattier side up, in foil-lined roasting pan. Score a diamond pattern in the fat with a Sharpe knife, about ¼ to ½ inches deep. And the parallel lines about 1 ½ apart. Do not score the meat itself, just the fat and any skin. You can score the fat to as deep as where the fat meets the meat. If you want you can first cur off and skin that might still be on the ham, but it isn't necessary

3. If using clove (with the sweet honey mustard Glaze), you can either put them in before applying the glaze or after. They look better if applied after, but it is easier to see the line on the ham as a guide for placement if you put them in first. Place clove in the center of the diamonds to form a nice pattern around the top and sides of the ham. (Some people put cloves in the intersection points of the score. Do as you wish. You just warn a nice pattern

4. Prepare glaze if using the sweet honey mustard glaze, mix the mustard with brown sugar in a small bowl. If using the honey thyme glaze, mix thyme in with melted butter and let sit for a few minutes. In a small saucepan on high heat, let cider vinegar reduce down from ¼ cup to 1 tablespoon, remove from the heat. Whisk in the butter and thyme. Add the honey, the brown sugar, and Worcestershire sauce

5. Using a pastry brush, brush whichever glaze you using over the ham. Only use about third of the glaze (reserve the rest for later in cooking). Try to work the glaze into the scored lines

6. Place ham in oven. Cook for about 1 ½ hours (check after one hour, will take longer if the ham is not at room temperature to begin with), or about 10 minutes per pound, until the internal temperature of the ham is 110 to 120 degree (use a meat thermometer). (Note that the ham is already cooked when you buy it, all you are trying to do is to heat it up for eating.) Baste the ham with the glaze a

couple of time during the cooking. If you check on the ham and think that the glaze is at risk of getting too browned (like on the way to burnt), you can cover with a piece of foil

7. When the ham has reached the desired temperature, finish it off in the boiler for minutes or two just to get some nice browning on the top. Take the pan out of the oven and brush the ham all over with pan juices. Cover with aluminum foil and let rest for 15 minutes before serving

8. To slice a bone-in ham, cut around the bone first. Then use a long, sharp knife to slice off piece around bone.

Remember to <u>save the ham bone for soup!</u>

Easily serve a dozen with leftovers

Glazed Oxtails

Ingredients

4 Lbs of oxtails

Kosher salt

¼ Cup grape seed or olive oil

2 Cups of onion chopped

½ Cup celery chopped

½ Cup carrot chopped

2 Tbsp olive oil

1 750ml bottle full bodied red wine

4 Cups veal, beef, or chicken stock

1 Teaspoon dried thyme

Freshly ground pepper

Directions

1. 2 Tbsp oil in a 5 to 6 quart thick bottomed Dutch oven on medium high heat. Working in batches, pat dry the oxtail with paper towels, sprinkles them on all sides with kosher salt, and add them to the pan, fat side down on the pan. Add more oil as needed with each batches of oxtail. Do not crowd the pan. Let them get well browned on one side before using tongs to move them. Brown well on all sides. Remove to a large bowl

2. Add the onions, carrots, to the pan. Sauté until translucent and lightly browned, about 5 minutes. Remove the vegetables from the pot to a bowl, cover and set aside

3. Add the bottle of wine to the pot. Increase the heat to as high as it will go, scraping up any browned bits from the bottom of the pan. Boil the wine, uncovered, until it is reduce to about cup

4. Return the oxtail back to the pot (but not vegetables). Add the stock and enough water to just cover them. Add the thyme, bring to a boil and reduce to a simmer, covered. Simmer on the stovetop for 3 hours. (You can also place the simmering oxtails into a 350 degree oven for the same amount of time if the oven is more convenient.) Add the vegetable back to the pot when you have about a half left to go

5. Remove from the heat and let chill in the refrigerator overnight so that the flavors blend and the fat on the surface solidifies, making it easier to remove. You can skip this step, but oxtail will be better if they are chilled in this state overnight

6. The next day, remove the pot from the refrigerator and scrape off the layer of rendered fat that has solidified on the top of the oxtails. If you are not waiting for the oxtails to chill, the fat still needs to be removed. If working with room temperature or warn pot, use a fat separator or a large metal spoon to skim off the fat

7. Heat the oxtail on medium heat. Cook uncovered for about another half an hour, or until the meat can be pulls ed off the bones. Then use a slotted spoon to remove the oxtail of the pot. Let cool enough to tough. Use your hands to remove the meat from bones to a bowl. Take care to remove as well around the cartilage caps on either end of the vertebrae

8. (optional, if you want a smoother glaze) While the oxtail is cooling in the step above, stain the mixture in the pot discarding the solids and returning the liquid to the pot. Increase the hear to high to bring the liquid to a boil

9. When the liquid has reduced by about a half, add the oxtail meat back in to the pot. Bring to a boil; continue to a boil away liquid until it has reduced to a light syrupy consistency. As the mixture

boil down, you may want to reduce the heat to a simmer, and stir the oxtails a little so that the glaze doesn't burn and so that the meat doesn't stick to the pan. When the right consistency, remove from heat and serve.

Yield: serve4-5

Mom Meatloaf

Ingredients

1 ½ lbs ground beef

¾ Cup cornflake, crushed

1 egg, slightly beaten

½ Cup milk

½ tablespoon salt

½ teaspoon pepper

¼ Cup onion chopped

Ketchup

Directions

1. Mix all ingredients (except ketchup) well and shape into loaf
2. Spread ketchup over the top
3. Bake for about 2 hour at 250 degree

New England Boiled Dinner

Ingredients

3 ½ lbs corned beef brisket or plain beef brisket

15 peppercorns

8 whole cloves

1 bay leaf

Kosher salt if you are use a beef brisket

2 medium sized turnips, peeled and quartered

4 red new potatoes, peeled and quartered

3 large carrots cut into thirds and the thickest pieces quartered lengthwise

1 small head cabbage, cut into fourths

Directions

1. Put the brisket in a 5 or 6 quart Dutch oven and cover with an inch of water. If you are using corned beef brisket and it does not come already packed in seasoning, add peppercorn, cloves, and 1bay leaf to the pot. If using a plain brisket, add a teaspoon of kosher salt for every quart of water. Bring to a simmer and then cover; lower the heat until it is barely simmer. Keep at a low simmer for 4 hour or until the meat is tender (a fork goes through easily).

2. Remove the meat and set side, keeping the meat warm. Add the vegetables to the pot. Check the broth for taste. If it too salty, add a little more water to taste. Raise the temperature and bring the

soup to a high simmer. Cook at a high simmer until done, about 15-30 minutes longer, depending on the size of the cut of your vegetables

3. Slice the meat in thin slices against the grain. You may find it easier to slice if you first cut the brisket in half along the same direction as the grain of the meat. Then slice smaller lengths against the grain. Serve in bowls a few pieces of meat in each; add some of the vegetables and some broth. Serve with horseradish or mustard or both.

Yield: Serves 6 to 8

Oxtail Stew

Ingredients

3 lbs oxtail with separated joints

Kosher salt and ground pepper

Olive oil

1 medium yellow onion, chopped

1 celery rib, chopped

1 large carrot, chopped

2 Cups of stock (chicken or beef)

2 Cops of red wine

3 whole cloves garlic, peel still on

1 bay leaf

Pinch of thyme

Parsley

2 carrots cut into 1-inch segments, large pieces also cut lengthwise

2 parsnips cut into 1-inch segments, large pieces also cut lengthwise

2 turnips cut into 1-inch pieces

Olive oil

Kosher salt and ground pepper

Directions

1. Preheat oven to 350 degree. Pat dry oxtail with paper towel. Sprinkle oxtail all over with kosher salt and ground pepper. Heat 1 tablespoon of olive oil on medium to medium high heat in a 6 quart Dutch oven. Working in batches, and not crowding the pan, sears the oxtail in hot pan on all side until golden brown. Using tongs to remove oxtail to a plate, setting side

2. Add the chopped onion, carrot, and celery to the pan. Cook for a few minutes until onions are translucent. Add the oxtails back to the pan. Add the cloves garlic, the stock and wine. Add bay leaf, thyme and half a teaspoon of salt. Bring to simmer, reduce heat to low cover and cook for 3 hours, until meat is fork tender.

3. One hour before the meat is done, heat oven to 350 degree. Toss carrots, parsnips, and turnips in olive oil in a roast pan. Sprinkle with kosher salt and ground pepper. Roast vegetables for one hour, or until lightly browned and cook through

4. When meat is tender, remove oxtails from the cooking liquid. Ether skim the fat off the top with a spoon, use a fat separator to remove the fat, or chill the cooking liquid for several hours so that the fat solidify, making it easier to remove. If you are making ahead, at this point you just put the stew in the refrigerator (let come to room temp first), with the oxtail still in it, and let it chill over night. The next day, scrape off the fat, and then remover the meat from the dish

5. Pour the cooking liquid through a mesh strainer into a bowl, using a rubber spatula to press against the vegetable solids caught in the strainer. Discard the solids. Return the liquid back to the pan and simmer until reduced by half. Then add the oxtails, and add the roast vegetables to the pan. Heat on low heat for half and hour for the flavors to meld. Add some chopped parsley before serving

Yield 4-6 serves

Pork Chops

Ingredients

4 pork chops

1 Teaspoon of bacon fat or olive oil

Kosher salt

1-2 Teaspoon dry rub*

*Dry rub

¼ Cup cumin seeds

3Tablespoon whole black peppercorns

1 Tablespoon coriander seeds

2 Tablespoon sugar

1 ½ Teaspoon kosher salt

1. Combine cumin, peppercorns, and coriander in a heavy medium skillet. Stir over medium heat until fragrant and toasted, about 8 minutes. Cool slightly; finely grind toasted spice in blender. Transfer to a small bowl. Mix in sugar and kosher salt. Mix makes ½ cup

Directions

1. Heat a large cast iron frying pan to medium high or high heat (hot enough to sear the meat). While the pan is heating, sprinkle

a pinch of dry rub spices (about 1/8 teaspoon or a little more) on each side of the pork chops. Using your fingers, rub the spice into the meat. Turn the chops over and repeat on the other side

2. Once the pan is hot, add a teaspoon of oil or fat to the pan and coat the bottom of the pan. Right before you put the chops into the pan sprinkle each side with a little salt, or you can salt the chops in the pan. Put the chops in the pan. Make sure they are not crowding each other too mush. There should be space between the chops in the pan or the meat will steam and not sear properly *

3. Sear the chops, about 2 minutes on each side. Watch carefully, as soon as the chops are browned, flip them. As soon as you flip the chops if you are using a cast iron pan, you can turn off the heat. Cast iron holds heat very well and there will be enough heat in the pan to finish cooking the meat. If you chops that are a lot thicker than ¾ inch (many are sold that are 1 ½ inch thick), you can put a cover on the pan and let chops finish cooking for 5 minutes or so if you using a cast iron pan and have turned off the heat, there should be enough heat if you cover the pan to finish the cooking of a thicker chop, if not, lower the heat to low and cover

4. How do you know when the chops are done? You can use the touch test which with practice I've leaned as well. If you wait until you se juice oozing out of the top of the chop, it is definitely done. Typically just keeps the chops in the pan, the heat is turned off, so the pan is losing heat. The pan initially provides enough not to searing the meat. After a couple of minutes, it's just keeping the chops warm

* Tip: Arrange the chops in the pan with the thickest, boniest parts toward the center of the pan where they get most heat

Yield serves 4-6, depending on the thickness of the chops

Pot Roast

Ingredients

3 ½ lb of beef shoulder or boneless chuck roast (look for a pieces that is well marbled with fat for best results)

2 Tbsp olive or grape seed oil

Kosher salt, ground pepper, Italian seasoning

2 large yellow onion, thickly sliced, lengthwise (root to tip), about 4 cups sliced onion

4 cloves of garlic, peeled

½ cup of red wine

1 bay leaf

Several carrots, peeled and lengthwise

Directions

1. Use a thick-bottomed cover pot (oven-proof if you intend to cook in oven), such as a Dutch oven, just large enough to hold roast and vegetable. Heat 2 Tbsp of oil on medium high heat (hot enough to sear the meat). Pat the roast dry with paper towels. Sprinkle and rub kosher salt, pepper, and Italian seasoning all over the meat. Brown roast in pot, all over, several minutes on each side. Don't move the roast while a side is browning, or it won't brown well

2. When roast is browned, remove from pan and set on a plate. Add the onions to the pan and cook for about 5-10 minutes, until they bring to brown. Add the garlic and carrots to sit on top of the onions.

Set the roast on top of the onions, garlic, and carrots. Add ½ cup of red wine. Add the bay leaf, cover. Bring to simmer and then adjust the heat down to the lowest heat possible to maintain a low simmer when covered (we cook our roast and warn setting of our electric ranger)*. If cooking in oven, start the temp. at 300degree for 15 minutes, then drop it to 200degree

3. Cook for 3 ½ to 4 hours, or longer, until meat is tender, (If you are using a pressure cooker, cut the time by half). After cooking for 3 ½ hours. Note how much liquid has been released by the meat. This comes from slow cooking at a low temperature. If your pot roast is to dry, make sure the pan you are using has tight fitting lid and that you are cooking at the lowest possible heat to maintain the low simmer

*If you are using a gas range, you may find difficulty getting the flame low enough. A tip I lean is take aluminum foil roll up in a tightly and shaping it into a skinny donut, and putting that on top of the burner to create little more distance between the ranges and the pan. If you have one of those high BTU ranges, I recommend cooking the roast in the oven instead

Yield serves 4-5

Roast Beef

Ingredients

3 to 3 ½ lbs of boneless rump roast (pick an end cur with a layer of fat if you can)

Olive oil

8 slivers of garlic

Kosher salt and ground pepper

For the gravy

Red wine, water, and or beef stock

Corn starch

Directions

1. Start with the roast at room temperature (remove from refrigerator one hour before cooking—keep it wrapped). Preheat the oven to 375 degree.

2. With a sharp knife make 8 small incisions around roast Place a sliver of Garlic into each incision. Take a tablespoon or so of olive oil and spread all around the roast. Sprinkle around roast with kosher salt and ground pepper. Place the roast directly on an oven rack, fatty sides up, with a drip pan on a rack beneath the

roasting rack. This arrangement creates convection in the oven so that you do not need to turn roast. The roast is placed fat up side up so that as the fat melt it will bathe entire roast in it juices

3. Brown the roast at 375 degree for half an hour. Lower the heat to 225dergee. The roast should take somewhere from 1 ½ to 2 ½ hours additionally to cook. The shape of the roast will affect the cooking time, by the way. So if your roast is on the long and narrow side, versus a more round shape, it may take less time to cook. So keep an eye on it. When the roast just starts to drip its juices and it are is brown on the outside, check the temperature with a meat thermometer. Pull the roast from the oven when the inside temperature of the roast is 135 degree. Let the roast rest for at least 15 minutes, tented in aluminums foil to keep warm, before carving to serve.

Gravy Brown

Remove the dripping pan from the oven and place on the stove top at medium heat. Note that if you are pulling the roast early, for rare or a medium rare level of doneness, you may not have a lot of dripping. Hopefully you will have some. If not, you may want to leave the roast in a little longer at a even lower heat 175 degree to ease some more dripping out of it.

Shepherd's Pie

Ingredients

1 ½ lbs ground round beef

1 onion chopped

1-2 Cups vegetable chopped carrots, corn peas

1-1 ½ lbs Potatoes (3 big ones)

8 tablespoon butter (1stick)

½ Cup beef broth

1 Teaspoon Worcestershire sauce

Kosher salt, pepper,

Directions

1. Peel and quarter potatoes, boil in salt water until tender (about 20 minutes).
2. While the potatoes are cooking, melt 4 tablespoon (½ stick) in a large frying pan
3. Sauté onion in butter until tender over medium heat (10 minutes). If you are adding vegetables, add them according to cooking time. Put any carrot in with the onion. Add corn or peas either at the end of the cooking of the onions, or after the meat has initially cooked

4. Add ground beef and sauté until no longer pink. Add kosher salt and pepper, add Worcestershire sauce. Add half a cup broth and cook. Covered, over low heat for 10 minutes, adding more beef broth as necessary to keep moist

5. Mash potatoes in bowl remember of butter, season to taste

6. Place beef and onions in bake dish. Distribute mashed potatoes on top. Rough up with a fork so that there are peaks that will brown nicely. You can use the fork to make some designs in potatoes as well.

7. Cook in 400 degree oven until bubbling and brown (about 30 minutes). Broil for last few minutes if necessary to brown.

Spareribs and Sauerkraut

Ingredients

2 lbs of bone-in pork spareribs (about ½ a pound per person)

1 large (28 oz) can of sauerkraut

1 large yellow onion, peeled and copped

1 Cup white wine

Water

Kosher salt and pepper

Directions

1. Sprinkle kosher salt and pepper on the ribs. Put ribs, sauerkraut. Onion, and wine into a large saucepan. Add just enough water to cover the ribs.
2. Bring to a boil and reduce heat to a simmer. Simmer until the meat falls off the bones, anywhere from one to two hours, Remove bones

Serves 4

DESSERT

Apple Crisp

Ingredients

7 Tart apples, peeled, core and slice

4 Teaspoon fresh lemon juice

½ Teaspoon vanilla

1 Cup brown sugar

½ Teaspoon ground cinnamon

1 Cup rolled oats

½ Cup butter, room temperature

Direction

1. Preheat oven to 375 degree. In a mixture bowl, combine apples, lemon juice, and vanilla. Toss to combine

2. Layer slice apples in a 9x12 inch (or approximately the same size) baking pan

3. Combine brown sugar, cinnamon, and oatmeal in a bowl. Cut in the butter. Sprinkle sugar mixture over apples

4. Bake for 45 minutes or until topping looks crunchy and the apples are tender

Serve 8 whipped cream or vanilla ice cream

Apple Upside Down Cake

Ingredients

8 Tbsp (one stick) unsalted butter, softened

1 ¼ Cups white, Granulate sugar divided (½ cup and ¾ cup)

1 ½ pounds brae burn, Jonagold or Golden Delicious apple (about 4 medium) peeled, quartered, cored each quarter cut into 2 wedges **

¾ Cup flour

½ Teaspoon salt

2 Teaspoons baking powder

1/3 Cup cornmeal

½ Cup boiling water

1 Teaspoon vanilla extract

2 Large eggs

1/3 Cup whole milk

1 9-inch cake pan with 1 ½ inch high sides

Direction

1. Preheat your oven to 350 degree. Butter the sides of the cake pan. Line the pan with a 10-inch round of parchment paper. The paper will come up ½- inch up the sides of the pan. Butter the parchment paper

2. Melt 2 tbsp butter in a non-stick skillet on medium heat. Add ½ cup sugar and cook until sugar dissolves and mixture turns golden brown, stirring occasionally (use a wooden spoon), about 6 minutes. Add apple wedges to the pan and gently stir to distribute the caramel evenly across the apples. Cover the pan and cook until apples release their juices, about 5 minutes. Uncover and cook until apples are tender and caramel thickens and coats the apples, stirring occasionally, about 13 minutes more. Remove apples and caramel sauce and place in the prepared cake pan

3. Whisk together the flour, kosher salt and baking powder in a small bowl and set side. Place cornmeal in a large mixture bowl. Pour ½ cup boiling water over cornmeal and stir to blend. Add 6 tbsp (¾ stick) butter to the cornmeal mixture. Beat until well blended. Beat in Vanilla and eggs. Beat in the flour, kosher salt, baking powder mixture alternating with milk. Pour the batter over the apples in the cake pan

4. Bake until top is golden and a tester inserted into the center come out clean, about 40 minutes. Cool cake in the pan for 5 minutes. Then run a knife around the edges of the cake to loosen it from the sides of the pan. Carefully invert the cake onto a serving plate or dish, and remove the parchment paper. Cool for 15 minutes

Make 6 to 8 servings. Serve with vanilla ice cream

** you can also use Pineapple

Apple Pie

Ingredient

Pastry for 2 crusts (recipe below)

8 Cups sliced, peeled baking apples—about lbs.

2 Tablespoon lemon juice

¾ Cup white sugar

¼ Cup brown sugar

¼ Cup all-purpose flour

¼ Teaspoon ground nutmeg

1 Teaspoon ground cinnamon

2 Tablespoon butter

1 Egg yolk

1 Tablespoon milk

Direction

1. In a large bowl, toss the sliced apple with lemon juice
2. Combine sugars, flour, cinnamon and nutmeg, add to apples and toss well to coat
3. Fill pastry lined 9 inch pie pan with apple mixture. Dot with butter
4. Place second crust on top of the pie filling, cut slits in top of crust vent. Seal the edges of the crust with a fork or by hand

5. In a small bowl, beat the egg and milk. Brush over the top of crust

6. Bake at 425 Degree F for 15 minutes

7. Reduce heat to 350 Degree F and bake for 40-45 minutes more or until crust is golden brown and the filling is bubby

Flaky Pastry Pie Crust Recipe

Ingredients

2 ½ Cups all-purpose flour

½ Teaspoon salt

1 Cup butter, chilled and diced

½ Cup ice water

Directions

1. Combine the flour and in a large bowl
2. Cut in the butter until the mixture resembles coarse crumbs
3. Stir in ice water, a tablespoon at a time, until the crush forms a ball
4. Wrap dough in plastic wrap and refrigerate for 4 hours or overnight
5. Sprinkle flour onto rolling surface. Roll dough out, and then divide in half. Roll each half to fit a 9-inch pie plate
6. Place crust in pie plate, pressing evenly into the bottom and side

Baked Apple

Ingredients

4 large good baking apples, such as Rome beauty, golden delicious, or Jonagold

¼ Cup brown sugar

1 teaspoon cinnamon

¼ chopped pecans

¼ Cup currants or raisins

1 tablespoon butter

¾ boiling water

Direction

Preheat oven to 375 degree. Wash apples. Remove cores to ½ inch of the bottom of the apples. If helps if you have an apple core, but if not, you can use a paring knife to cut out first the stem area, and then the core. Use a spoon to dig out the seeds. Make the hole about ¾ inch to an inch wide

In a small bowl, combine the sugar, cinnamon, currants/ raisins, and pecans. Place apples in an 8x8 inch square baking pan. Stuff each apple with this mixture. Top with a dot of butter (¼ of tablespoons).

Add boiling water to the baking pan. Bake 30-40 minutes, until tender, but not mushy. Remove from the oven and baste the apples several times with the pan juices

Serve warm with vanilla ice cream on the side

Yield makes 4 servings

Blackberry Cobbler

Berry mixture

4 C ups blackberries, rinsed clean

½ Cup sugar (less or more to taste, depends on how sweet the berries are and how sweet you would like your cobbler to be)

1 Teaspoon lemon zest

1 tablespoon lemon juice

¼ teaspoon cinnamon

1 ½ tablespoon cornstarch or (for thickening, can use instant tapioca instead)

Cobbler topping

3 tablespoon sugar

1 Cup all purpose flour

1 ½ teaspoon baking powder

¼ teaspoon salt

4 tablespoon butter

¼ cup milk

1 Egg, lightly beaten

Direction

1. Place berries, sugar, lemon zest, lemon juice, cinnamon, and cornstarch in a 9x9 casserole dish. Stir to coat the berries evenly with the sugar. Let sit for 30 minutes

2. Preheat oven to 350 degree. In a medium sized bowl, whisk together 3 tablespoon of sugar, the flour, baking powder, and salt. Cut butter in with a pastry blender or fork or even your finger) until the mixture resembles coarse crumbs. Use a wooden spoon to sir in the egg and milk until the batter is lust moistened

3. Taking spoonfuls drop the batter mixture over the berries. Place in the oven and bake for 30 minutes or until the berry mixture is bubbly and the topping is nicely browned

Great serve with whipped cream or vanilla ice cream

Yield: makes 9 servings

Blackberry Pie

Ingredients

<u>Pie dough recipe</u> for top and bottom crust

5-6 cups <u>blackberries,</u> rinsed, picked clean, patted dry (if you use frozen berries, defrost and drain them)

½ cup to ¾ cup sugar (depending on how sweet your berries are)

1 teaspoon lemon juice

1 teaspoon lemon zest

½ teaspoon ground cinnamon

¼ teaspoon almond extract

3 tablespoon quick cooking instant tapioca (can usually find in the baking aisle of your local supermarket)

Direction

1. Place blackberries, sugar, lemon, zest, lemon juice, cinnamon, almond extract, and quick cooking instant tapioca in a large bowl. Gently fold the berries until they are all well coated with sugar. Let sit for 30 minutes

2. Preheat oven to 400 degree. You should have two balls of pie dough, one for the bottom crust, one for the top crust. Roll out of the balls of pie dough on a lightly floured surface to a 12 inch diameter if you are using a 9 inch pie pan or 13 inch diameter if you using a 10 inch pan. Line the bottom of your pie pan with the dough. Chill in refrigerator while you roll out the bottom crust

3. Roll out the second ball of pie dough for the top crust. If you would like to do a lattice top, weave the dough stripe as described in How to make a lattice top for a pie crust

4. Spoon the berry mixture into the dough-lined pie dish. For a lattice top, weave stripes of pie dough over the top of the fruit-filled pie dish. For a solid top, place the second roll-out pie dough crust on top of the pie. Press ends of the strips into the rim of the bottom crust. Use scissors to trim the edges to ½-inch from the outer edge of the pie pan. Fold that edges back over themselves and use your finger to crimp to seal the edges. If you are using a solid top crust, score the top with a sharp knife to create air vents for the steam to escape

5. Place the pie on the middle rack of the oven. Put a baking sheet on the lower rack to catch any juices that might bubble out of the pie while it's cooking. Bake the pie in two stages. First bake it at 400 degree for 30 minutes. Then place a sheet of aluminum foil over the pie to protect the edges and tops from getting too burnt. (A pie protector is quite useful here.) Reduce the heat to 350 degree and bake for additional 30 minutes, until crust has browned and the filling is bubbly

Remove and oven and place on a wire rack. Cool completely before serving Yield Makes 8 servings

Bread Pudding

Bourbon Sauce

½ Cup (1 stick) butter, melted

1 Cup sugar

1 Egg

1 Cup Kentucky bourdon whiskey

Bread Pudding

Loaf French bread, at least day old, cut into one-inch squares (about 6-7 cup)

1 Qt milk

3 Egg, lightly beaten

2 Cups sugar

2 Tbsp vanilla

1 Cup raisins (soaked overnight in ¼ cup bourdon)

¼ teaspoon allspice

¼-½ teaspoon cinnamon

3 Tbsp unsalted butter, melted

Direction

In a saucepan, melt butter; add sugar and egg, whisking to blend well. Cook over low heat, stirring constantly, until mixture thickens. (Do not allow simmering, or it may curdle.) Whisk in bourdon to taste. Remove from heat. Whisk before serving. The sauce should be soft. Creamy and smooth.

Bread Pudding

1. Preheat oven to 350 degree.

2. Soak the bread in milk in a large mixture bowl. Press with hands until well mixed and all the milk are absorbed. In a separate bowl, beat eggs, sugar, vanilla and spices together. Gently stir into the bread mixture. Gently stir the raisins into the mixture

3. Pour butter into the bottom of a 9x13 inch baking pan. Coat the bottom and the sides of the pan well with the butter. Pour in the bread mix and bake at 35-45 minutes, until set. The pudding is done when the edges start getting a bit brown and pull away from the edge of the pan can also make individual ramekins

Serve with bourbon whiskey sauce on the side, pour on to taste. Best fresh and eaten the day it is made. Makes 8-10 servings.

Old Depression brown cake

Ingredients

1 Cup water

2 Cup raisins

1 Tsp. cinnamon

½ Tsp. cloves

1 Cup brown sugar

1/3 Cup lards (shortening)

¼ Tsp. nutmeg

¼ Tsp. salt

2 Cups flour

1Tsp. Baking soda

½ Tsp. baking powder

Direction

Place water, raisins, cinnamon, cloves, brown sugar, lard (shortening), nutmeg and salt in a saucepan and mix. Place on heat and bring to a boil. Cook 3 minutes. Allow to cool, then sift together the flour, bake soda and baking powder. Stir into cooked mixture.

Place in a greased Loaf pan and bake 350 degree for one hour.

Lemon Meringue Pie

Ingredients

1 Cup white sugar

2 tablespoon all-purpose flour

¼ teaspoon cornstarch

1 ½ cups water

2 Lemon, Juiced and zested

2 tablespoons butter

4 egg yolks, beaten

1 (9inch) pie crust, baked

4 egg whites

6 tablespoons white sugar

Directions

1. Preheat oven to 350 degrees
2. To make lemon filling: In a medium saucepan, whisk 1 cup sugar, flour, cornstarch, and salt. Stir in water, lemon juice and lemon zest. Cook over medium high hest, stirring frequently, until mixture comes to a boil, stir in butter. Place egg yolk in a bowl and gradually whisk in ½ cup of hot sugar mixture. Whisk egg yolk mixture back into remaining sugar mixture. Bring to a boil and continue to cook while stirring constantly until thick. Remove of the heat. Pour filling into baked pastry shell.

3. To make meringue: In a large glass or metal bowl, whip egg whites until foamy. Add sugar gradually, and continue to whip until stiff peaks form. Spread meringue over pie, sealing the edges at the crust.

4. Bake in preheated oven for 10 minutes, or meringue brown.

Old fashion peach Cobbler

Ingredients

2 ½ Cups All-propose flour

3 Tablespoon white sugar

1 Cup shortening

1 Egg

¼ Cup cold water

3 pounds fresh peaches—peeled, pitted and sliced

¼ Cup Lemon juice

¾ Cup orange juice

2 Cups white sugar

½ Cup butter

½ teaspoon ground nutmeg

1 teaspoon ground cinnamon

1 Tablespoon cornstarch

1Tablespoon white sugar

1 Tablespoon butter, Melt

Directions

1. In a medium bowl, sift together the flour, 3 tablespoons sugar, and
    salt. Work in the shortening with a pastry blender until the mixture
    resembles coarse crumbs. In a small bowl, whisk together the egg

and cold water. Sprinkle over flour mixture, and work with hands to form dough into a ball. Chill 30 minutes

2. Preheat oven to 350 degrees (175 degree c). Roll out half of dough to 1/8 inch thickness. Place in a 9x 13 inch dish, covering bottom and halfway up sides. Bake for 20 minutes or until golden brown

3. In a large saucepan, mix the peaches, lemon juice, and orange juice. Add ½ cup butter, and cook over medium-low heat until butter is melted. In a mixing bowl, stir together 2 cups, nutmeg, cinnamon, and cornstarch, mix into peach mixture. Remove from heat, pour into baked crust

4. Roll remaining dough to thickness of ¼ inch. Cut into half-inch-wide strips. Weave strips into a lattice over peaches. Sprinkle with 1 tablespoon sugar, and drizzle with 1 tablespoon melted butter

5. Baked in preheated oven for 35 to 40 minutes, or until top crust is golden brown

MEASUREMENT

Liquid or Volume Measurement

Jigger or measure	1 1/2 or 1.5 fluid ounces		3 Tablespoons	45 ml
1 Cup	8 fluid ounces	1/2 pint	16 Tablespoons	237 ml
2 cups	16 fluid ounce	1 pint	32 Tablespoons	474 ml
4 cups	32 fluid ounce	1 quart	64 Tablespoons	.946 ml
2 pints	32 fluid ounce	1 quart	4 cups	.964 liters
4 quarts	128 fluid ounces	1 gallon	16 cups	3.8 liters
8 quarts	256 fluid ounces or one peck	2 qallons	32 cups	7.5 liters
4 pecks	one bushel			
dash	less than 1/4 Teaspoon			

Dry/Weight Measurement

		Ounces	Pounds	Metric
1/16 Teaspoon	a dash			
1/8 Teaspoon	a pinch or 6 drops			.5ml
1/4 Teaspoon	15 drops			1ml
1/2 Teaspoon	30 drops			2ml
1 Teaspoon	1/3 Tablespoon	1/6 ounce		5ml
3 Teaspoon	1 Tablespoon	1/2 ounce		14 grams
1 Tablespoon	3 Teaspoons	1/2 ounce		14 grams
2 Tablespoon	1/8 cup	1 ounce		28 grams
4 Tablespoon	1/4 cup	2 ounce		56.7 grams
5 tablespoon plus 2 Teaspoon	1/3 cup	2.6 ounce		75.6 grams
8 Tablespoon	1/2 cup	4 ounce	1/4 pound	113 grams
10 Tablespoon plus 2 Teaspoon	2/3 cup	5.2 ounces		151 grams
12 Tablespoons	3/4 cup	6 ounces	.375 pound	170 grams
16 Tablespoon	1 cup	8 ounces	1/2 pound	225 gram
32 Tablespoon	2 cup	16 ounces	1 pound	454 gram
64 Tablespoon	4 cups or 1 quart	32 ounces	2 pounds	907 gram

www.ingramcontent.com/pod-product-compliance
Lightning Source LLC
Chambersburg PA
CBHW031247120626
46545CB00007B/2694